HANDEL

Acis and Galatea

A serenata for soprano, 2 tenors & bass soli
SATB & orchestra

Edited by Joseph Barnby
Revised by Watkins Shaw, 1974

Order No: NOV 070122

NOVELLO PUBLISHING LIMITED

CONTENTS

PART I

REVISER'S INTRODUCTION

As Sir Joseph Barnby clearly stated in the Preface originally printed with this edition, all the choruses save one ('Happy we') are arrangements for SATB, with occasionally divided sopranos and tenors, of Handel's original scoring for STTTB. At the present time, when authenticity of text is valued, and rightly so, the question arises whether Barnby's arrangement is acceptable. Given that a mixed four-part chorus cannot reproduce the characteristic sonority of the original all male five-part scoring, he did his work with skill and judgment. Careful comparison reveals that he has not materially damaged Handel's counterpoint or spoiled the flow of the individual lines; and, on the footing that it makes a lovely work much more widely available than could otherwise be, Barnby's work may be commended.

Only in bars 9-11 of p. 104 has any amendment to his adjustment of the voice parts seemed called for, though minor corrections have been made in the text, and 19 bars have been restored to No. 30, as explained in Note 5 below.

Handel's violin and oboe accompaniments often follow, for long stretches, the contour of the chorus parts, and it is here that a less skilled arrangement than Barnby's might have raised conflict. As it is, this marries well with the unaltered instrumental parts, except that an octave adjustment to the second violin for half a bar at letter C of the first chorus seems required and has now accordingly been made.

The chorus 'Happy we', a later addition to the work as originally composed, was written by Handel for SATB and is given unchanged.

Notes

1   A good deal of rhythmic alteration is required in performance. For example, many weak quavers should be shortened, such as those following a quaver rest or a dotted crotchet on pp. 13-14, 20-22, and 70-71. On p. 22 the semiquavers after the shake (bar 2, etc.) will be postponed and become demisemiquavers. The accompaniment in the second half of bar 5 on p. 95 should be  These instances should be sufficient to indicate the treatment.

2   Cadential shakes should be introduced into the orchestral parts.

3   Solo singers will find it natural to introduce the traditional *appoggiature* into the recitatives, for example: as well as cadential shakes and other appropriate graces in the arias, though graces are perhaps out of place in 'O ruddier than the cherry'.

4 The aria 'Would you gain the tender creature' appears in the early sources sometimes in F, sometimes in G. From a note in Handel's original manuscript, indicating where this aria should come (but without the music), it would appear just possible that he may have thought of it as alternative to 'Cease to beauty to be suing', although word-books contemporary with him print both.

5 In the autograph score a 'cut' of 19 bars in the final chorus has been marked, presumably by Handel, and Barnby worked from a version lacking these bars. They have now been restored, should it be desired to use them, in a form congruent with his SATB texture. They are not found in the first published score, issued by Walsh in 1743, and the MS score now in the Staats- und Universitätsbibliothek, Hamburg has marks where pieces of paper were at one time fixed to make the excision. My own opinion is that the movement is better without these bars.

6 Any marks of style not found in the original source but supplied by Barnby have now been placed in square brackets. All the dynamic and metronome marks are Barnby's.

This is not the place to discuss the complicated history of *Acis and Galatea*, valuable information about which may be found in *Concerning Handel* (Cassell & Co., 1948) by William C. Smith.

The prime source of text lying behind this edition is Handel's autograph score in the British Library (formerly the British Museum Library), RM 20.a.2, which now lacks the final 17 bars. In this, the earliest form of the work,* Part I ended with the duet 'Happy we' without the chorus (pp. 41-43), and No. 19 was not included. For the 'Happy we' chorus, the text has been checked against RM 18.c.11 in the British Library, and other passages not found in the autograph have been checked against ADD. MSS 5321, 31561, 36710, and Egerton MS 2940 in the British Library, Music MS 792 in the Fitzwilliam Museum, Cambridge, and MS MUS. 185 in the Staats- und Universitätsbibliothek, Hamburg.

WATKINS SHAW 1974

*Composed 1718. See Terence Best's letter in *The Musical Times*, vol. 113 (1972), p. 43.

Orchestral material is available on hire.

SINFONIA.

4

CHORUS.—"O THE PLEASURE OF THE PLAINS."

9

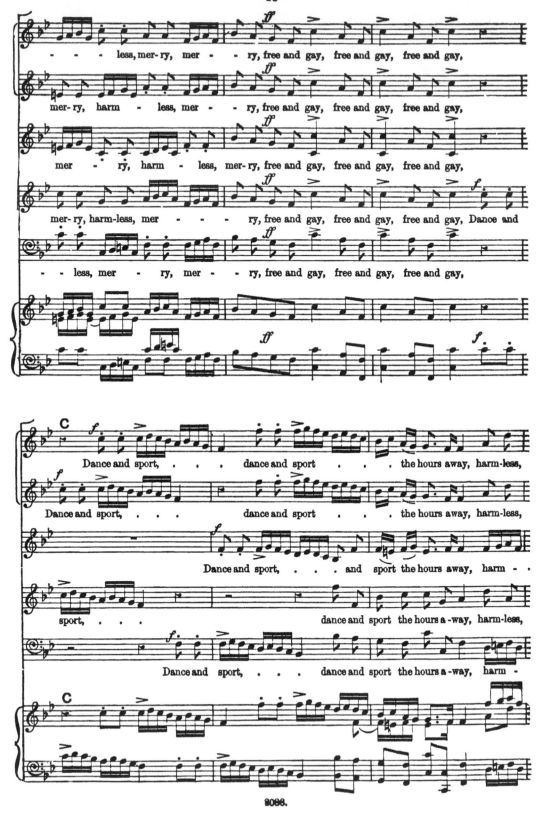

For us the zephyr blows, For us dis-tils the dew, For us un-folds the rose, And flow'rs dis-play their hue,

For us the zephyr blows, For us dis-tils the dew, . . For us unfolds the rose, And flow'rs display their

For us the zephyr blows, For us unfolds the rose, And flow'rs . . display their

For us the zephyr blows, For us dis-tils the dew, And flow'rs . . display their

For us the zephyr blows, For us dis-tils the dew, For us unfolds the rose, And flow'rs display their

* Handel gives this to Tenor II. See note on rhythmic alteration in preliminary matter.

14

8088.

GALATEA. *

Hush,

hush,   ye pretty, pretty warb - ling choir; Your thrill- ing strains a-wake my pains,   And

8088.

pls

19

Cease your song, and take your flight, Bring back my A - cis to my sight, bring back my A - cis to my sight, Cease your song, and take your flight, cease your song, ... and take your flight, Bring back my A - cis, bring back my A - cis to my sight.

This song may be shortened by beginning the repeat at the sign *
and omitting the 16 bars between the two signs †

Air.—"WHERE SHALL I SEEK THE CHARMING FAIR?"*

* See note on rhythmic alteration in preliminary matter.

21

way, kind Ge - - - nius of the mount - ains, Where shall I

seek . . . . the charming fair?

Where, where, where, . . . where shall I seek the charm - ing

fair? Direct the way, kind Ge - nius of the mountains.

8088.

O tell me if you saw my dear, Seeks she the groves, or bathes in crys-tal fount-ains, O tell . . . . me, tell me if you saw my dear, Seeks she the groves, or bathes in crys-tal fount - ains? seeks she the groves, ... or bathes . . . in crys - tal fount - ains?

* The following eight bars of Symphony may be omitted.

8088.

24

DAMON.

Shep - herd, what art thou pur-su - ing,

shep - herd, what art thou pur-su - ing? Heed - less run - ning to thy

ru - in, heed - less run - ning to thy ru - in, Share our joy, our pleas - ure

share, share our pleas - - - - - - - ure, share our joy, . . our pleas - ure

share. Shep - herd,

8088.

Leave thy pas - sion till to - mor-row, Let the

day be free from sor - row, Free from love and free from care, free from

love and free from care, free from love and free from care.

FINE.

FINE. *p*

D.C.

D.C.

* The following nine and a half bars of Symphony may be omitted.

No. 8.

Lo ! here my love ! Turn, Ga - la - te - a, hi - ther turn thine eyes, See at thy feet, the long-ing A - cis lies.

No. 9. AIR.—" LOVE IN HER EYES SITS PLAYING."

Love in her eyes sits play - ing, And sheds de - li - cious death ; Love . .

C

... in her lips is stray - ing, And warb - ling in her breath,

Love in her lips is stray - ing, And warb - ling in her breath,

Love . . in her eyes sits

play-ing, love . . in her eyes sits play-ing, And sheds de - li - cious

death, Love . . in her eyes sits play - ing, love . . in her eyes sits

Love on her breast sits pant - ing, And swells with soft de - sire; No grace, no charm is want - ing, no grace, no charm is want - ing, To set the heart on fire, ... to set the heart on fire, No grace, no charm is want - ing, To set the heart on fire, No grace, no charm is want - ing, To set the heart on fire.

D.C. *

* The following six bars of Symphony may be omitted.

8088.

No. 10. RECIT.—"O DIDST THOU KNOW.

GALATEA.

SOPRANO.

O didst thou know the pains of absent love, A - cis would ne'er from Ga-la-te-a rove.

PIANO.

No. 11. AIR.—"AS WHEN THE DOVE LAMENTS HER LOVE."

Andante. GALATEA.

SOPRANO.

As when the dove la - ments her love, All on the

Andante.

PIANO. ♩=112.

na - ked spray,

As when the dove la -

- ments her love, All on the na - ked spray; When he tr re -

- turns, no more she mourns, But loves . . . the live-long day, ...

. . . . but loves the live-long day.

L.H.

As when the dove la-ments her

love, All on the na-ked spray, When he re-turns, no more she mourns, no

more she mourns, no, no, no,

When he re-turns, no more she mourns, But loves . . . . .

. . . . . the live - long day, When he re - turns

no more she mourns, But loves, ...

. . . . . but loves the live-long day.

FINE.

FINE.

Bill - ing, coo - ing,   Pant - ing, woo - ing,

p

Melt - ing mur - - - - - - - murs fill the grove, - - - -

p

. . . . melt - ing mur - - - - - - - murs, last - ing love,

Melt-ing mur - murs fill the grove, Melt - ing mur - murs, last - ing

Duet.—"HAPPY WE."

all . . my . . joy, Thou all . . my . . bliss, thou all . . my joy! What

p sempre.

joys . . I feel, Of all youth, thou dear-est boy !

What charms . . I see, Of all

Thou all . . my . . bliss, thou all . . my . . joy, thou

nymphs, thou bright-est fair ! Thou all . . my . . bliss, thou all . . my . . joy, thou

D.S.

all . . my . . bliss, . . thou all . . my joy !

all . . my . . bliss, . . thou all . . my joy ! *tr* Hap - py,

D.S.

* The rest of this Duet may be omitted and the Chorus joined on the end of this bar.

8088.

CHORUS.—"HAPPY WE."

PART THE SECOND.

CHORUS.—"WRETCHED LOVERS."

47

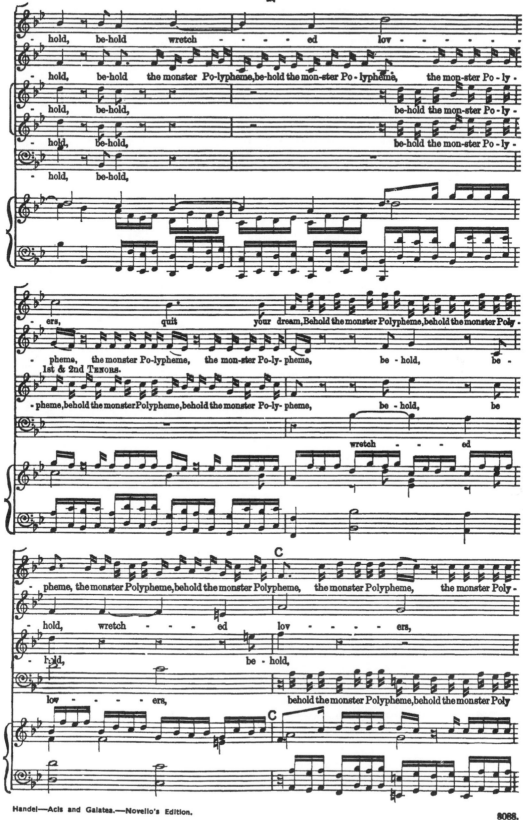

48

9088.

Ripe as the melt-ing clus-ter, No li - ly has such lus-tre, Yet hard to tame as
raging flame, And fierce as storms that blus-ter, Yet hard to tame as rag-ing flame, And fierce as storms that
blus -
- - ter, Yet hard to tame as rag - ing flame, And fierce as storms that
blus-ter. O rud-dier than the
p
f
p
D.S.
D.S.

RECIT.—" WHITHER, FAIREST, ART THOU RUNNING ? "

Whither, fair-est, art thou running ? Still my warm embraces shunning ! The li-on calls not to his prey, Nor bids the wolf the lambkin stay. Thee, Po-ly-phemus, great as Jove, Calls to em - pire and to love ; To his pa - lace in the rock, To his dai - ry, to his flock, To the grape of pur - ple hue, To the plum of glos - sy blue, Wildings which ex-pect-ing stand, Proud to be ga-ther'd by thy hand. Of in-fant limbs to make my food, And swill full draughts of human blood ! Go, mon-ster ! bid some o - ther guest ; I loathe the host ; I loathe the feast.

AIR.—" CEASE TO BEAUTY TO BE SUING."

ing, ev - er whin -ing love dis - dain - ing, Cease to beau - ty to be su - ing; Ev - er whin - ing love dis - dain - - - ing, ev - er whin-ing love dis - dain - ing.

Let the brave their aims pur-su-ing, Still be con-qu'ring, not.. com-plain-ing, still.. be conqu'ring, not com-plain-ing,

Let the brave their aims pur-su-ing, Still be con-qu'ring, still.. be con-qu'ring, still be con-qu'ring, not com-plain-ing.

D.C.

D.C.

✳

✳ This Air may be shortened by omitting the following 15 bars, and commencing *dal segno*, †.

AIR.—" WOULD YOU GAIN THE TENDER CREATURE."

64

8088.

Soft - ly, gent - ly, kind-ly

treat her, Suff'ring is .. the lov-er's part.

FINE.

FINE.

Beau - ty, by con - straint, pos - sess - ing, You en - joy but half .. the

bless - ing, Life - less charms with - out the heart, life - less charms

with-out the heart, Beau-ty by con-straint, pos - sess - ing, You en -

- joy but half the bless - ing, Life - less charms with-out the heart.

D.C.

No. 20. **Recit.—"HIS HIDEOUS LOVE."**

TENOR. ACIS.

His hi-deous love provokes my rage; Weak as I am, I must en-

PIANO.

- gage; In-spir'd by thy vic-to-rious charms, The god of love will lend his arms.

AIR.—"LOVE SOUNDS THE ALARM."

* At the *Da Capo*, the 15 bars following this sign may be omitted.

8088.

When beau-ty's the prize, when beau-ty's the prize, What mor-tal fears dy-ing?

When beau-ty's the prize,

when beau-ty's the prize, What mor-tal fears dy-ing?

When beau-ty's the prize,

What mor-tal fears dy-ing? Love sounds th'a-larm,

love sounds th'a - larm,   love sounds th'a- larm,   And   fear is   a - fly . . . . .

- ing,   Love sounds th'a - larm,   .   .   love sounds th'a - larm,

And   fear is   a - fly- ing,   When beau-ty's the   prize, when

beau-ty's the   prize, What mor- tal fears   dy-ing?   When beau- ty's the

prize, What mor-tal fears dy-ing?

FINE. In de-fence of my treas-ure I'd bleed at each vein, With-out her no

pleas-ure, For life is a pain, With-out her no pleas-ure, with-out her no

pleas-ure, For life is a pain, ... for life is a pain.

D.C.

AIR.—"CONSIDER, FOND SHEPHERD.†

TENOR.

PIANO.

Con - sid - er, fond shep - herd, how fleet - ing's .. the pleas - ure, That

† See note on rhythmic alteration in preliminary matter.

flat - ters our hope,.. in pur - suit of the fair,

Con - sid - er, fond shep - herd,

how fleet - - - - - - ing is the

pleas - ure, That

flat - ters our hope, in pur - suit.. of.. the fair, that.. flat - -

* The following 22 bars may be omitted.

No. 24.   TRIO.—"THE FLOCKS SHALL LEAVE THE MOUNTAINS."

No. 25.   RECIT.—"HELP, GALATEA."

Chorus.—"MOURN, ALL YE MUSES."

the gen - tle A - cis, the gen - tle A - cis is no more,

the gen - tle A - cis, the gen - tle A - cis is no more,

the gen - tle A - cis, the gen - tle A - cis is no more.

the gen - tle A - cis, the gen - tle A - cis is no more,

no more, no more, the gen- tle A - cis is no more.

no more, no more, the gen- tle A - cis is no more.

no more, no more, the gen- tle A - cis is no more.

no more, no more, the gen- tle A - cis is no more.

(Voices alone.)

pp

SOLO AND CHORUS. – "MUST I MY ACIS STILL BEMOAN?"

stone,

SOPRANO.

Cease, cease, Ga-la-te-a, cease to grieve, cease, Ga-la-te-a, cease to

ALTO.

Cease, cease, Ga-la-te-a, cease to grieve, cease, Ga-la-te-a, cease to

TENOR.

Cease, cease, Ga-la-te-a, cease to grieve, cease, Ga-la-te-a, cease to

BASS.

Cease, cease, Ga-la-te-a, cease to grieve, cease, Ga-la-te-a, cease to

Must I my A - cis still be-moan, In - glo - - rious crush'd, in -

grieve, cease, Ga-la-te-a, cease to

grieve, cease, Ga-la-te-a, cease to

grieve, cease, Ga-la-te-a, cease to

grieve, cease, Ga-la-te-a, cease to

glo - - - - - - - - - - - - - rious

grieve, cease, Ga-la-te-a, cease to grieve, cease, Ga-la-te-a, cease to

grieve, cease, Ga-la-te-a, cease to grieve, cease, Ga-la-te-a, cease to

grieve, cease, Ga-la-te-a, cease to grieve, cease, Ga-la-te-a, cease to

grieve, cease, Ga-la-te-a, cease to grieve, cease, Ga-la-te-a, cease to

crush'd be - - neath that stone, in - glo - rious crush'd be -

grieve, Be-wail not when thou canst re - lieve, be - wail not when thou canst re - lieve,

grieve, Be-wail not when thou canst re - lieve, be - wail not when thou canst re - lieve,

grieve, Be-wail not when thou canst re - lieve, be - wail not when thou canst re - lieve,

grieve, Be-wail not when thou canst re - lieve, be - wail not when thou canst re - lieve,

die,   die for his

cease, Ga - la - te - a, cease to grieve,   cease, Ga - la - te - a. cease to grieve,

cease, Ga - la - te - a, cease to grieve,   cease, Ga - la - te - a, cease to grieve,

cease, Ga - la - te - a, cease to grieve,   cease, Ga - la - te - a, cease to grieve,

cease, Ga - la - te - a, cease to grieve,   cease, Ga - la - te - a, cease to grieve,

con - - - - - stan - cy   and truth?

Be-wail not when thou canst re - lieve; Call forth thy pow'r, employ thy art; The god-dess

Be - wail not when thou canst re - lieve; Call forth thy pow'r, employ thy art; The god-dess

Be-wail not when thou canst re - lieve; Call forth thy pow'r, employ thy art; The god-dess

Be-wail not when thou canst re - lieve; Call forth thy pow'r, employ thy art; The god-dess

No. 28.   RECIT.—" 'TIS DONE."

SOPRANO.

GALATEA.

'Tis done: thus I ex-ert my pow'r di-vine;   Be thou im-mortal, tho' thou art not mine!

PIANO.

No. 29.   AIR.—" HEART, THE SEAT OF SOFT DELIGHT."

Larghetto.

PIANO.

GALATEA.

Heart, ... the   seat   of   soft   de - light, ...

. . . . .   Be   thou now   a . . .

fount - - -ain bright ! Heart, the seat of soft .. delight,

heart, the seat of soft .. delight, Be thou now a fount - ain

bright ! Pur - - ple be no more thy

blood, Glide thou like a crys - tal flood, glide thou like a

crys - tal flood, glide . . . .

thou like a crys - - - tal flood. Rock, thy hol - low womb dis-close: The bub - bling fount - ain, lo! it flows Through the plains he joys to rove, Murm' - ring still his gen - tle love, Through the

plains he joys to rove, Murm' -ring still his gen - tle love,

murm' - ring still his gen - tle love, murm' - ring still his gen - tle love, . . .

. . . murm'

. . ring, murm'ring still his gen - tle love.

Chorus.—"GALATEA, DRY THY TEARS."

SOPRANO.
Ga - la - te - a, dry . . thy tears, A - cis now a

ALTO.
Ga - la - te - a, dry . . thy tears, A - cis now a

TENOR.
Ga - la - te - a, dry . . thy tears, A - cis now a

BASS.
Ga - la - te - a, dry . . thy tears, A - cis now a

PIANO.
♩ = 96.

god ap - pears,

god ap - pears,

god ap - pears,

god ap - pears,

※ See note on rhythmic alteration in preliminary matter.

Optional cut. See Introduction.

Novello Publishing Limited

CHORAL WORKS
FOR MIXED VOICES

Bach   **Christmas Oratorio**
for soprano, alto, tenor & bass soli, SATB & orchestra

Mass in B minor
for two sopranos, alto, tenor & bass soli, SSATB & orchestra

St Matthew Passion
for soprano, alto, tenor & bass soli, SATB & orchestra

Brahms   **Requiem**
for soprano & baritone soli, SATB & orchestra

Elgar   **Give unto the Lord   Psalm 29**
for SATB & organ or orchestra

Fauré   **Requiem**
for soprano & baritone soli, SATB & orchestra
edited by Desmond Ratcliffe

Handel   **Messiah**
for soprano, alto, tenor & bass soli, SATB & orchestra
edited by Watkins Shaw

Haydn   **Creation**
for soprano, tenor & bass soli, SATB & orchestra

Imperial 'Nelson' Mass
for soprano, alto, tenor & bass soli, SATB & orchestra

Maria Theresa Mass
for soprano, alto, tenor & bass soli, SATB & orchestra

Mass in time of War 'Paukenmesse'
for soprano, alto, tenor & bass soli, SATB & orchestra

Monteverdi **Beatus Vir**
for soloists, double choir, organ & orchestra
edited by Denis Stevens & John Steele

Magnificat
for SSATB chorus, instruments & organ
edited by John Steele

Vespers
for soloists, double choir, organ & orchestra
edited by Denis Stevens

Mozart   **Requiem Mass**
for soprano, alto, tenor & bass soli, SATB & orchestra

Scarlatti   **Dixit Dominus**
for SATB, soli & chorus, string orchestra & organ continuo
edited by John Steele